WE CAN DRAW

WE CAN DRAW CARS

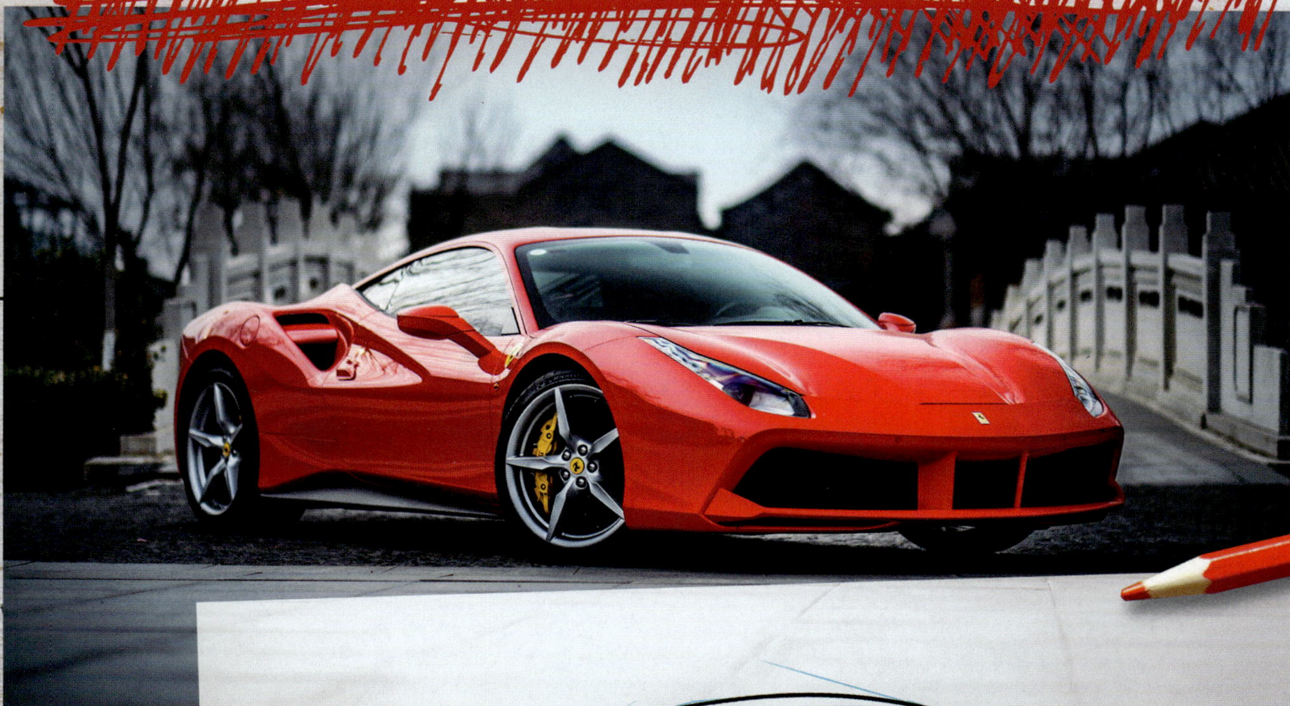

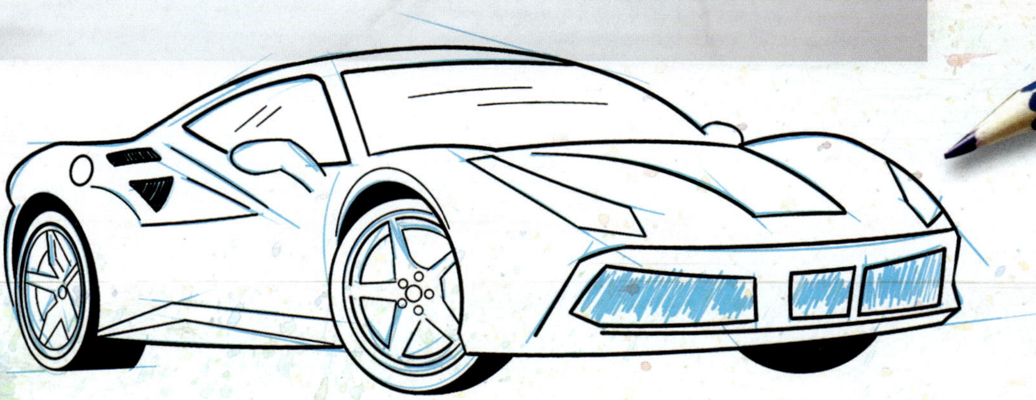

Corina Jeffries

WINDMILL BOOKS
New York

Published in 2023 by Windmill Books, an Imprint of Rosen Publishing
29 East 21st Street, New York, NY 10010

Portions of this work were originally authored by Laura Murawski and published as *How to Draw Cars*. All new material this edition authored by Corina Jeffries.

Library of Congress Cataloging-in-Publication Data
Names: Jeffries, Corina, author.
Title: We can draw cars / Corina Jeffries.
Description: New York : Windmill Books, [2023] | Series: We can draw | Includes index. | Audience: Grades 2-3
Identifiers: LCCN 2021054299 (print) | LCCN 2021054300 (ebook) | ISBN 9781508198024 (library binding) | ISBN 9781508198000 (paperback) | ISBN 9781508198017 (set) | ISBN 9781508198031 (ebook)
Subjects: LCSH: Automobiles in art–Juvenile literature. | Drawing–Technique–Juvenile literature.
Classification: LCC NC825.A8 J38 2023 (print) | LCC NC825.A8 (ebook) | DDC 743/.8962922–dc23/eng/20211209
LC record available at https://lccn.loc.gov/2021054299
LC ebook record available at https://lccn.loc.gov/2021054300

Designer: Leslie Taylor
Editor: Caitie McAneney

Photo credits: Cover, p. 1 (car) yousang/Shutterstock.com; series art (pencils) suriya yapin/Shutterstock.com; series art (brushes and table) insta_photos/Shutterstock.com; series art (banner) Kathy Kiselova/Shutterstock.com; series art (pencil shading background) mart/Shutterstock.com; p. 4 FernandoV/Shutterstock.com; p. 5 (pencils) ILLUSTOR STUDIO/Shutterstock.com; p. 5 (boy) Bangkok Click Studio/Shutterstock.com; p. 6 Carrie Fereday/Shuttertstock.com; p. 8 meunierd/Shutterstock.com; p. 10 https://commons.wikimedia.org/wiki/File:Revival04_005a.jpg; p. 12 Steve Lagreca/Shutterstock.com; p. 14 ATGImages/Shutterstock.com; p. 16 VanderWolf Images/Shutterstock.com; p. 18 JJ Aiston/Shutterstock.com; p. 20 https://commons.wikimedia.org/wiki/File:1999_Plymouth_Prowler_(15118085727).jpg.

Manufactured in the United States of America

CPSIA compliance information: Batch #CSWM23: For further information contact Rosen Publishing, New York, New York at 1-800-237-9932.

CONTENTS

YOU CAN DRAW CARS!

Think of your dream car. Even if you're not old enough to drive yet, you can imagine what kind of car you would want to drive. From **luxury** cars to race cars, these amazing machines are fun to learn about—and fun to draw!

Even though there are many kinds of cars, they all have the same basic parts, such as tires, engines, bumpers, and **fenders**. You can often tell which company made the car and when it was made by its special design. This book will teach you fun facts about eight exciting cars. Then, you can follow the instructions step by step to draw your own.

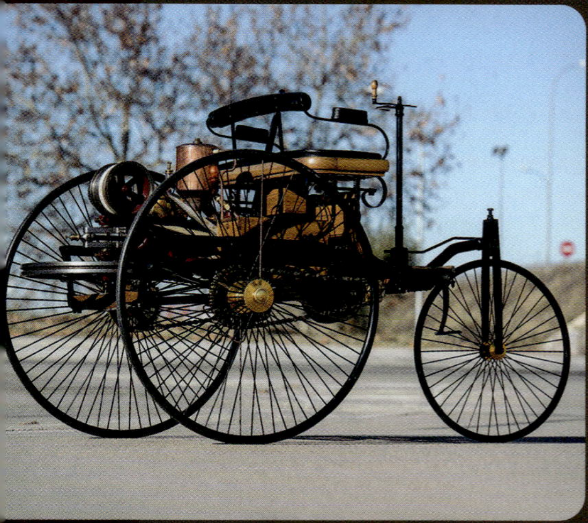

Some historic cars may look a little different from what you see today. That's true of the Benz Three-Wheeler—which had only three wheels! Notice the similarities and differences between the cars. As you follow directions, look at the illustration. Anything in color is a new step of the drawing process.

Gather your drawing materials!

You'll need a pencil, pencil sharpener, eraser, and paper. You might want to make your drawings in a sketch pad.

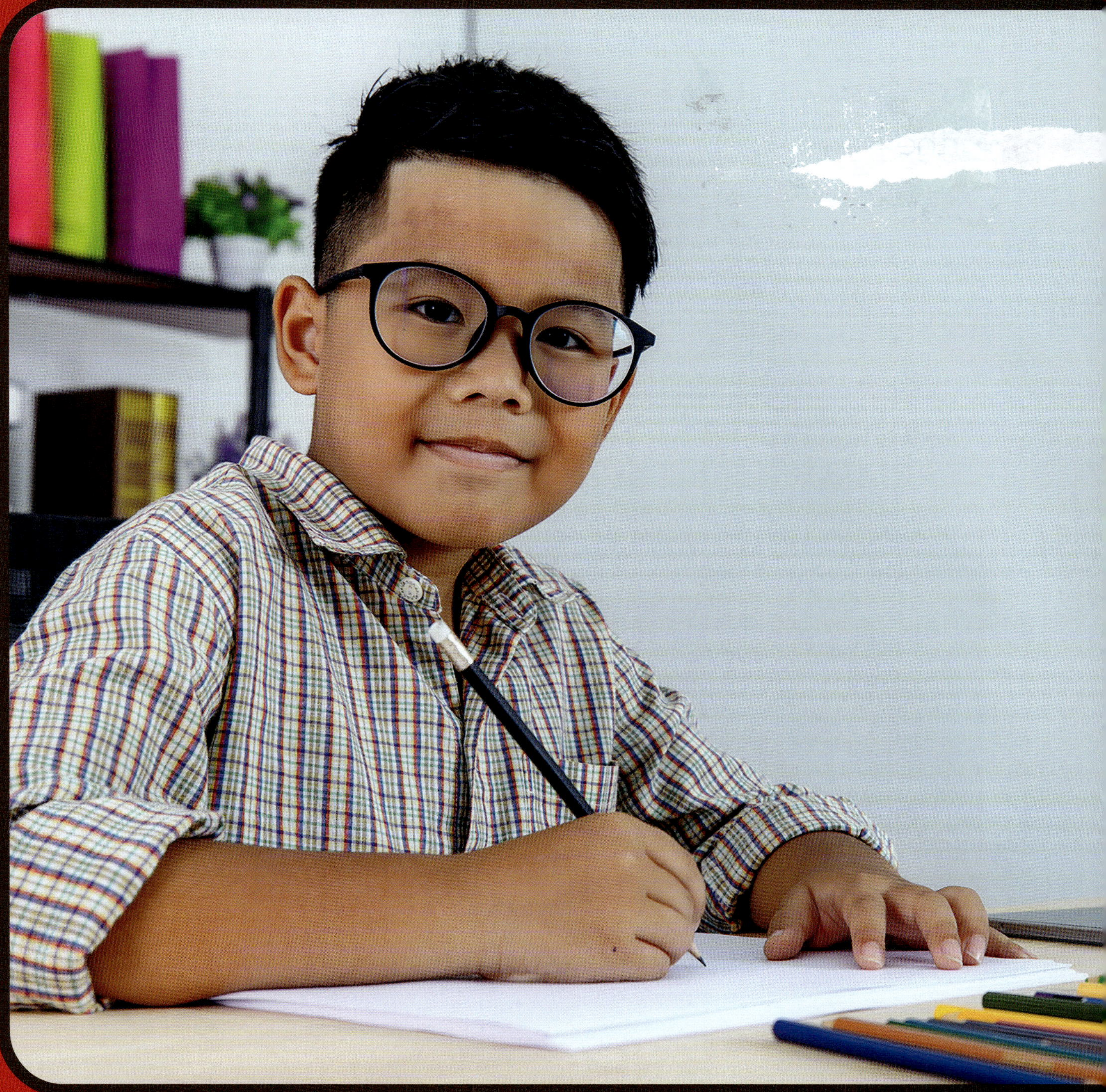

THE FIRST MOTORCAR

In 1885, Karl Benz, a German **engineer**, created what is often considered the first practical motorcar. Unlike the cars of today, this car had only three wheels, with two wheels in the back and one wheel in the front. It was sometimes called the Benz Tricycle.

Its engine was called a two-stroke engine, which made it go at a speed of only 8 miles (12.9 km) per hour. That speed is slow when you think about today's cars. Some cars can go up to 300 miles (482.8 km) per hour now! Like today's cars, this early car had a water-cooled engine, an electric **ignition**, and a **differential gear**. Look at its design to see how it compares to today's cars.

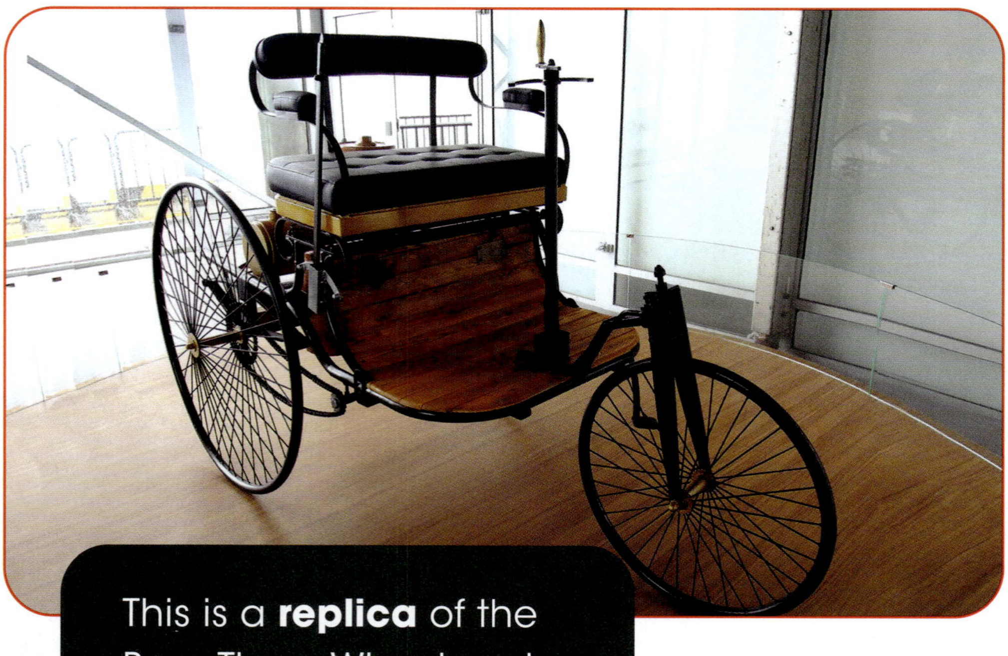

This is a **replica** of the Benz Three-Wheeler, also called the Benz Tricycle.

1

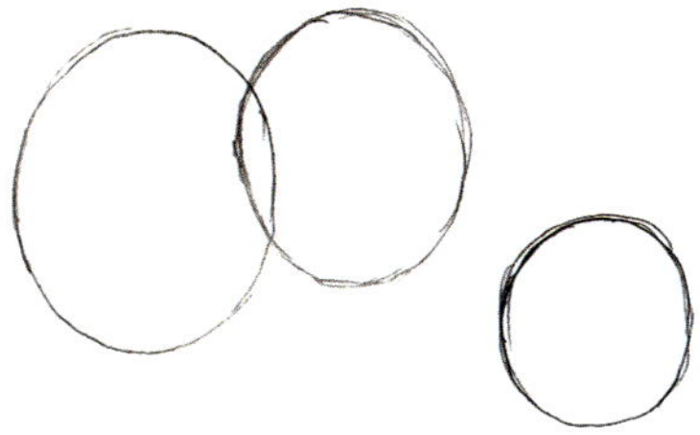

First, draw three circles for the wheels. Make the first circle larger than the one that crosses it. The third, and smallest, circle should be ahead of the first two, as shown here.

2

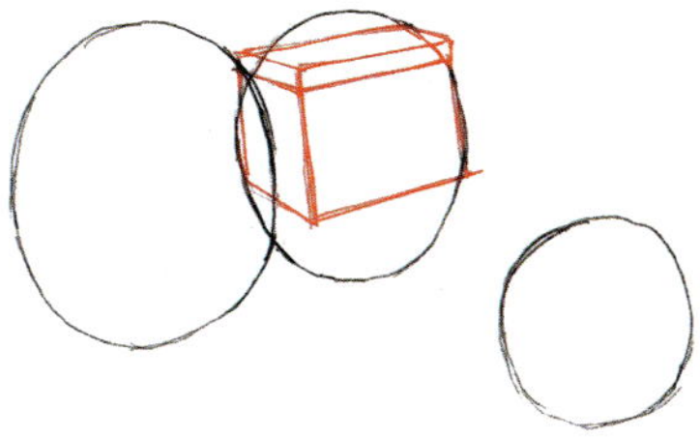

Now, draw a rectangle inside the middle circle. Draw a second rectangle a little higher and to the left of the first one. Draw two lines at both ends of the rectangles to join them. Then, add lines to the top of the box to make a lid.

3

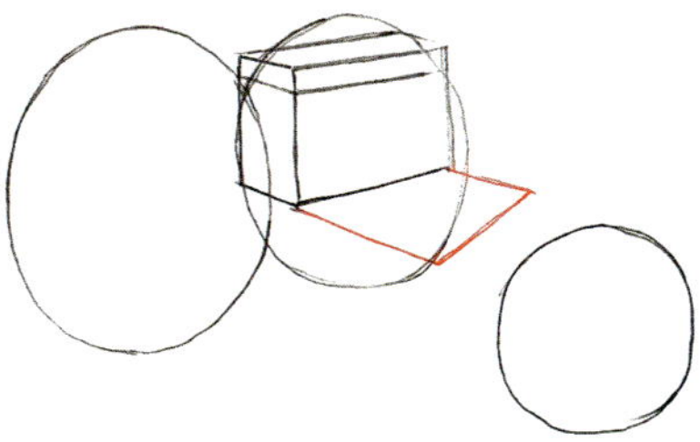

At the bottom of the box from Step 2, draw a rectangle with different-sized sides, as in the illustration.

4

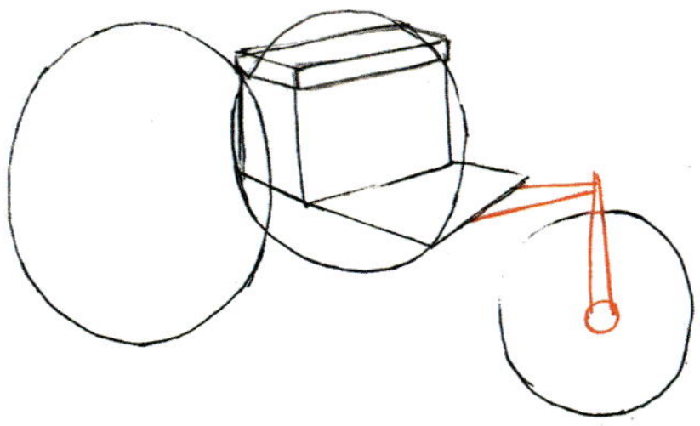

From the shape drawn in Step 3, draw two lines that come to a point. Now, draw two more lines that continue from that point. Notice how the two sets of lines meet at their points. Next, draw a tiny circle within the smallest circle, touching the vertical set of lines.

5

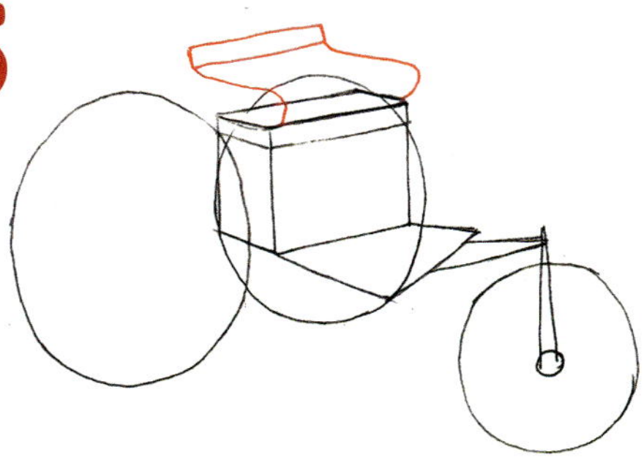

Then, draw two curved lines on top of the lid of the box from Step 2. Join them by adding a small rectangle at the top of the curved lines.

6

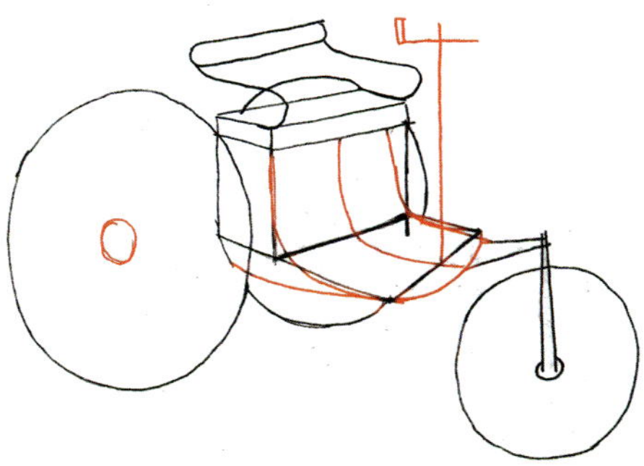

Lastly, curve the lines of the rectangle from Step 3 and the bottom of the box. Add a small circle to the biggest circle (wheel). Then, add a vertical line going up, starting at the bottom of the Step 3 rectangle. Add a horizontal line crossing the vertical line. Then, add the small handle at the left end of the horizontal line. Erase any extra lines. You've drawn a Benz Three-Wheeler!

THE FANTASTIC FORD MODEL T!

In 1908, Henry Ford made history when he introduced the Model T. In a 1922 race, Noel Bullock entered his Model T car, which he named "Old Liz." The car looked old and worn down. Many people said it looked like a tin can. This led to the Model T being nicknamed "Tin Lizzie." However, Bullock's car won the race—even against much more expensive cars!

Ford began the first **assembly-line** production of an entire car. Each worker was responsible for one task on a line. This working process made the Model T more affordable. Since it was also easy to drive and keep up, it became America's most popular car.

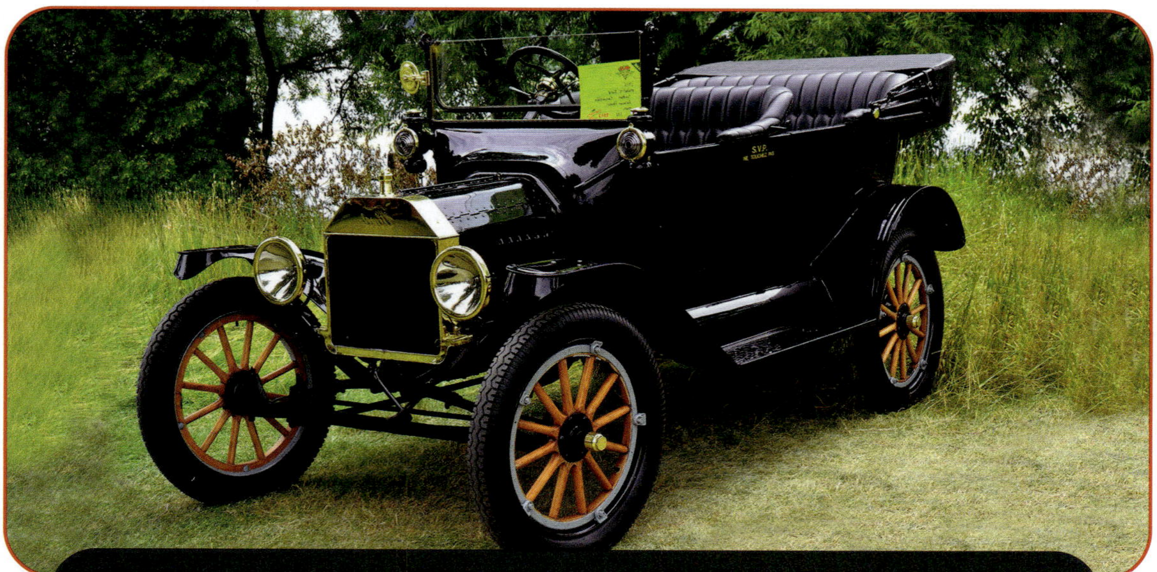

With the Model T car, Henry Ford changed the way cars were built.

1

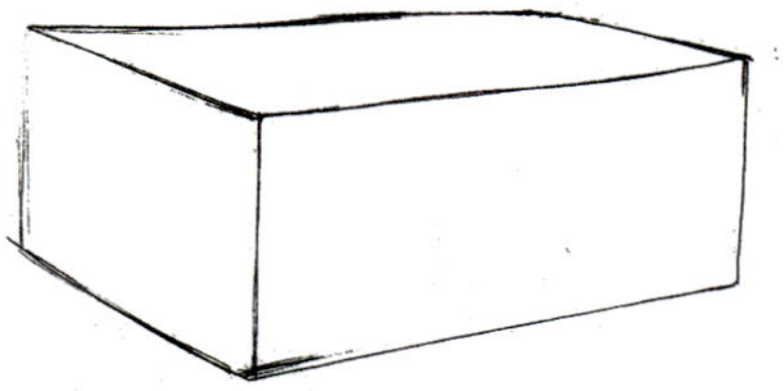

First, draw a 3-D box to guide your drawing.

2

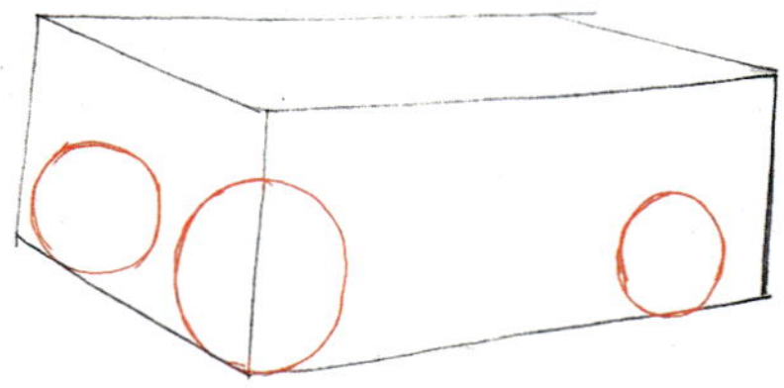

Next, draw three circles inside the box. Look at the illustration to see how big each circle should be and where they should be placed.

3

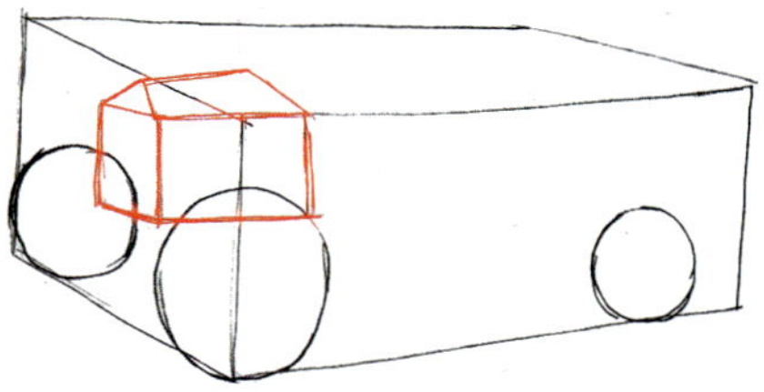

Draw a shape like a house at the front end of the box. This will be the front end and engine.

4

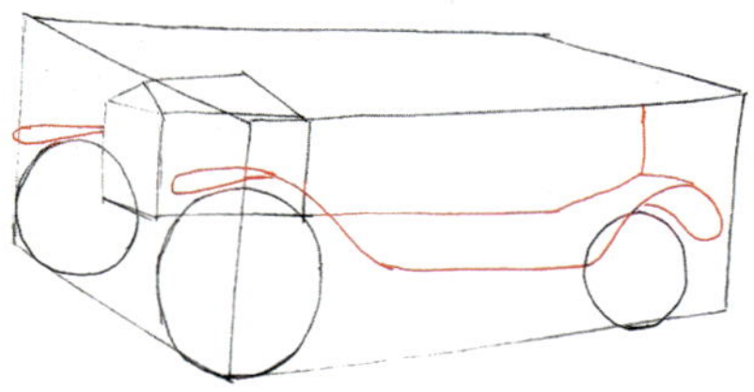

To form the body of the car, extend the bottom line of the house shape. Draw a long, curved line to make the fender. Draw two shapes like paddles above the two circles at the left to make the tops of the fenders.

5

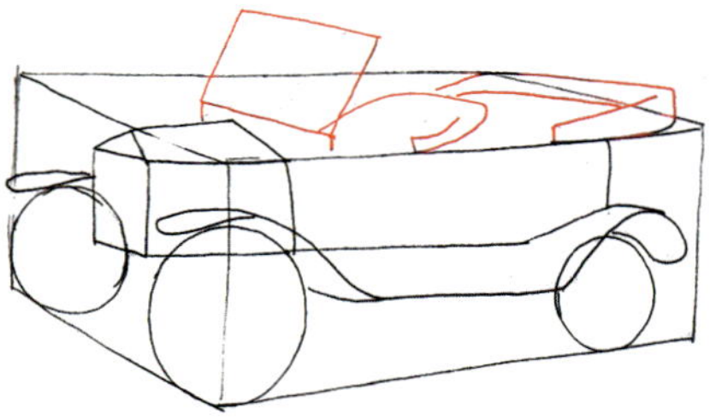

Draw the front window by making a slanted rectangle. Then, make two sets of curved lines behind the window to be the front and back seats.

6

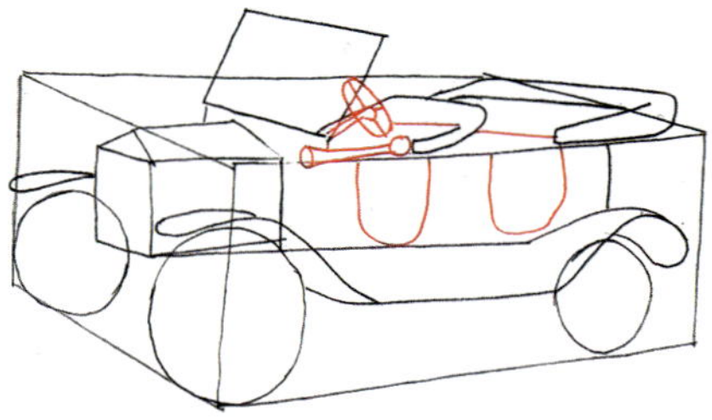

Look at the illustration to guide you as you draw in the details of the car. First, draw the steering wheel and the car horn. Draw in the two car doors by making two U shapes on the side of the car.

7

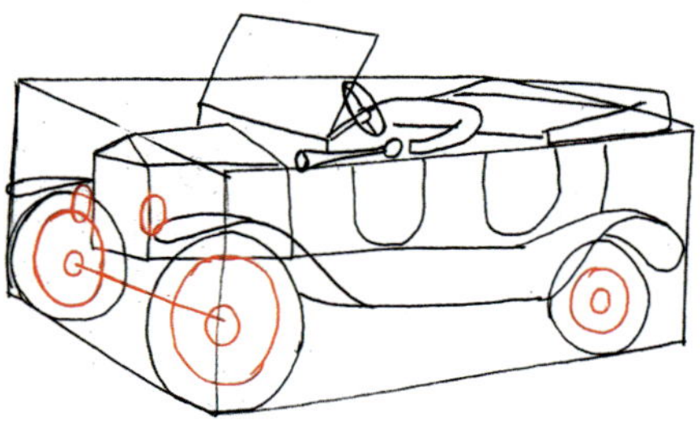

Then, draw two smaller circles within each of the larger circles (wheels). Connect the two smallest circles in the front wheels with a straight line. Next, add two small oval shapes at the front of the car for the headlights. These ovals should touch the paddle-shaped tops of the fenders.

8

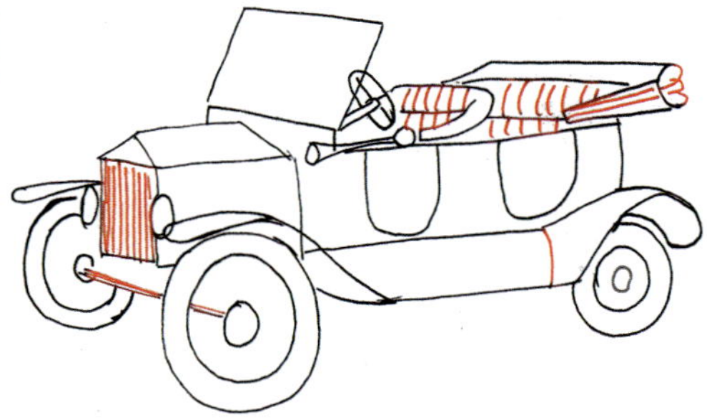

Lastly, add seven or eight vertical lines to the front **grille**. Then, add small curved lines to the seats. Add two slanted lines to the top of the back seat to make the hood. Erase any extra lines. You've now finished your Model T!

THE POWERFUL BUGATTI

The Bugatti 41 Royale was designed by an Italian-born Frenchman named Ettore Bugatti. As a teenager, Ettore studied art. However, he later became interested in making and racing motorcars. In 1898, he built his first car. Ettore began his own car company in 1910. He soon began to win races and became recognized for his race cars.

Ettore decided to build a luxury car. The Bugatti 41 Royale was the most powerful and **elegant** car of its time. This model of car was built from 1927 to 1933. It was also wildly expensive, so few people were able to afford it. The Bugatti 41 Royale was meant to be driven by a chauffeur, or a person hired to drive a car. Six were made, and only four were sold.

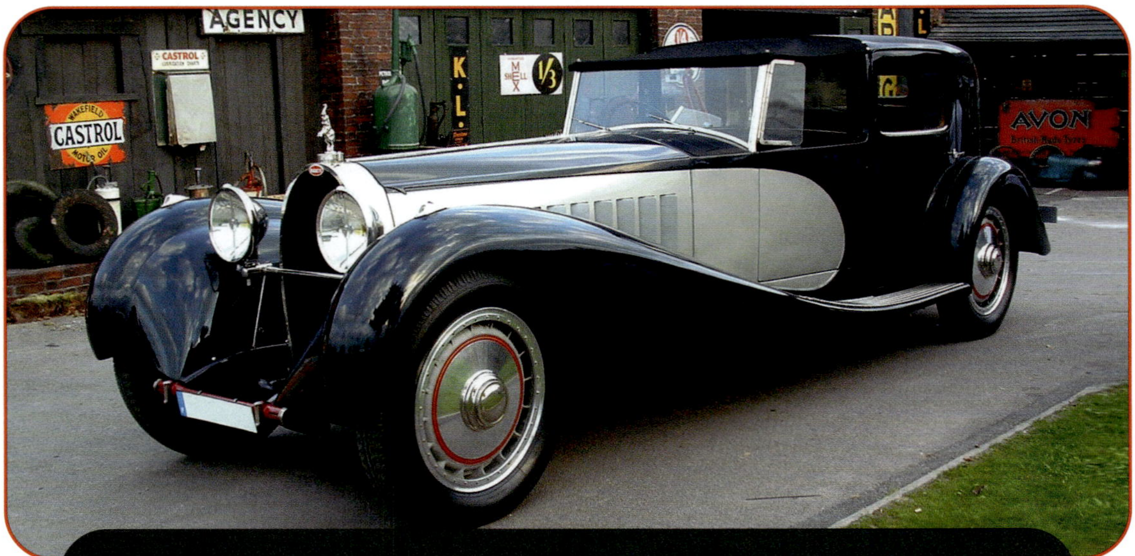

The Bugatti 41 Royale was a luxury car famous for its power—and its price.

1

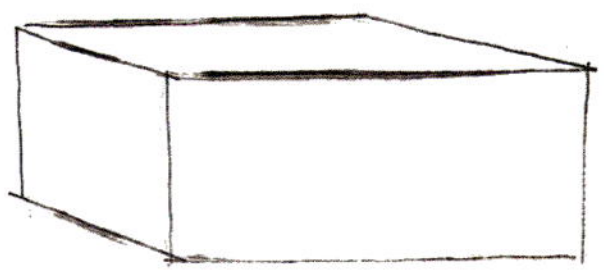

First, draw a 3-D box to guide your drawing.

2

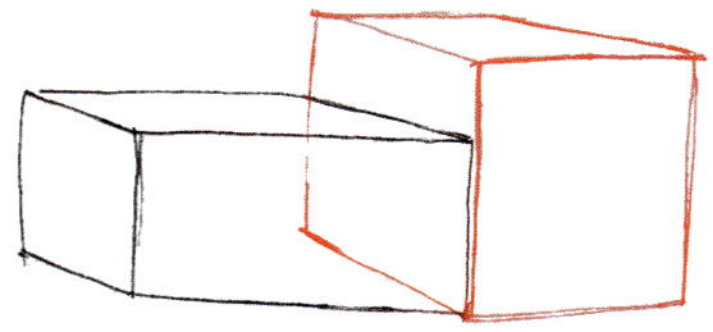

Draw a wider and taller box to the right of the first box. The boxes should be touching.

3

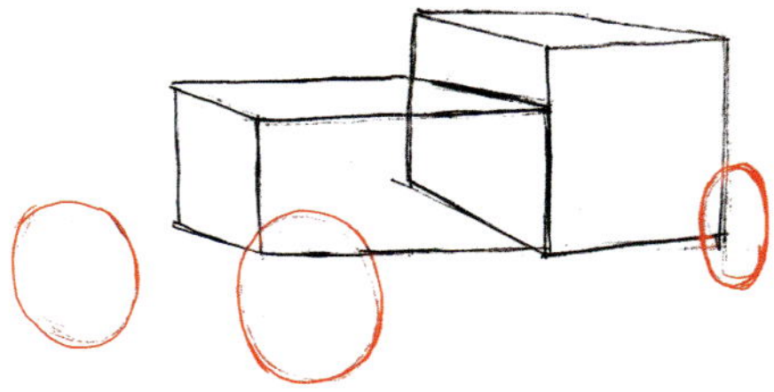

To make the wheels, draw three circles. The largest circle should touch the shortest box. Draw the second circle near the back corner of the shortest box. Add the third, smallest circle at the right corner of the tallest box.

4

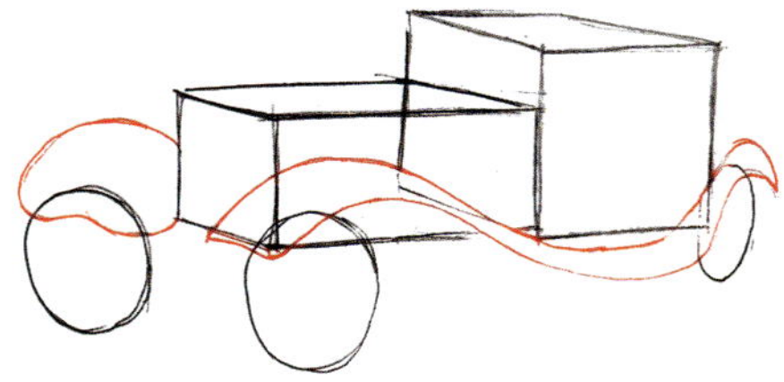

To make the fender, draw curved lines along the side of the car, as shown in the illustration. Then, add a shape that looks like a large kidney bean to the circle at the far left. This will be the fender on the other side of the car.

5

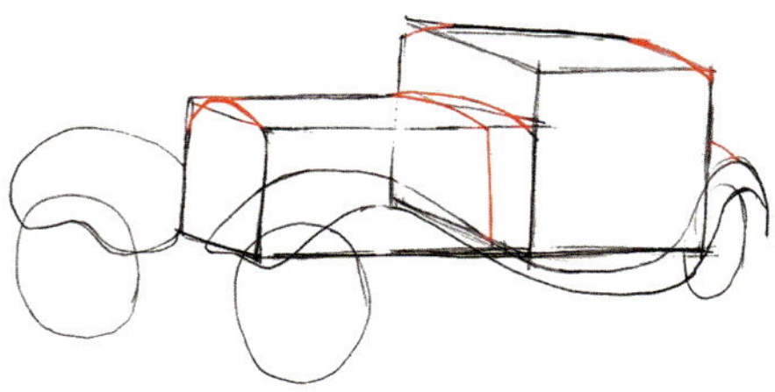

Next, make the top corners in both of the boxes rounded, or curved. Next, add a curved line on the side of the shorter box as shown here.

6

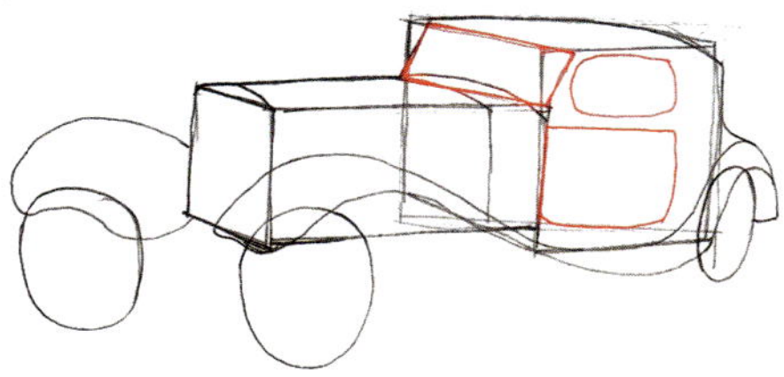

Add a rectangle to the top of the side of the tallest box. Notice how this rectangle slants. Draw a second rectangle on the side of the tallest box, but near the top. This rectangle should have rounded corners. Add a third, wider rectangle below the rounded one.

7

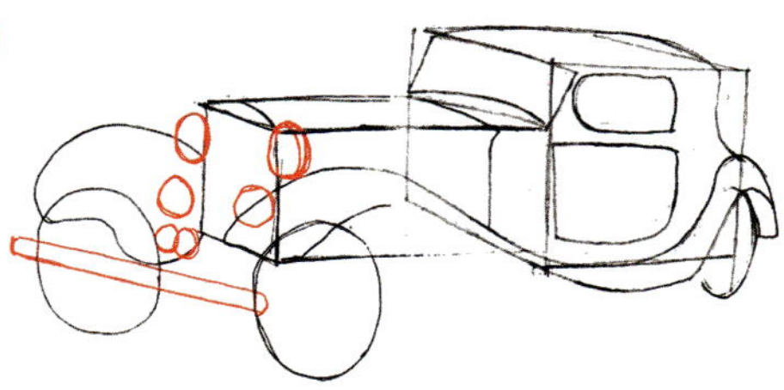

To make the car's headlights and horns, draw six more circles at the right of the shortest box, as shown here. Now, draw a long, thin rectangle that touches the two circles of the wheels at the right. This shape, which is the bumper, is placed at the front of the car.

8

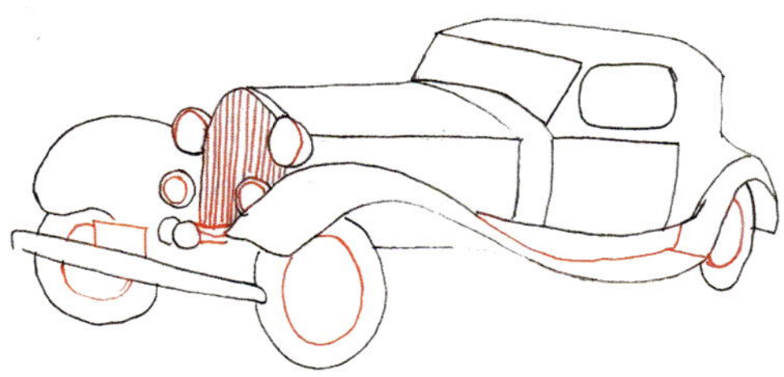

To complete the car's wheels, draw circles within each of the three circles. Add vertical lines to make the car's grille. Draw a small rectangle on top of the bumper to make the license plate. Add one more curved line along the fender, below the rectangle that is the car door. Now, you can erase any extra lines. You've just created your own luxury car fit for royalty!

THE V-8 ENGINE LEGEND

The legendary Bel Air Sport Coupe raced onto the automobile scene in 1955. What made the Bel Air so special was its V8 engine, which helped the car reach 93 miles (149 km) per hour. The V8 engine had a few nicknames, such as "Turbo-Fire" and the "Hot One."

In the first year it was built, the Bel Air won many car races, including one for the National Association for Stock Car Auto Racing (NASCAR). The Bel Air did so well as a racing car that it was chosen to be the official pace car for the world-famous Indianapolis 500 race. A pace car is a non-competing car that leads competing cars through a pace lap, but doesn't take part in the race itself.

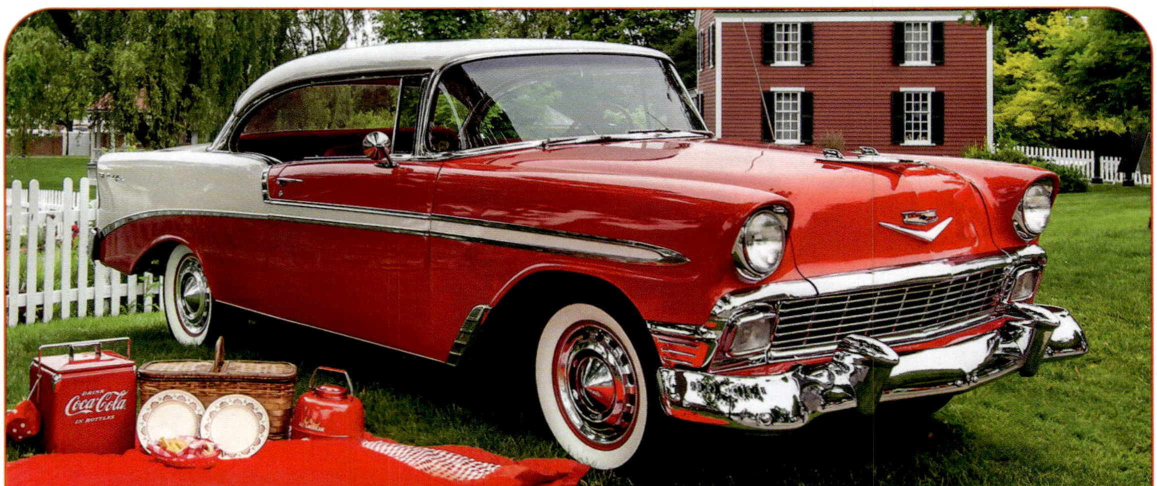

Chevrolet is a division of General Motors, started by Louis Chevrolet and William C. Durant in 1911. This is Chevrolet's Bel Air Sport Coupe.

1

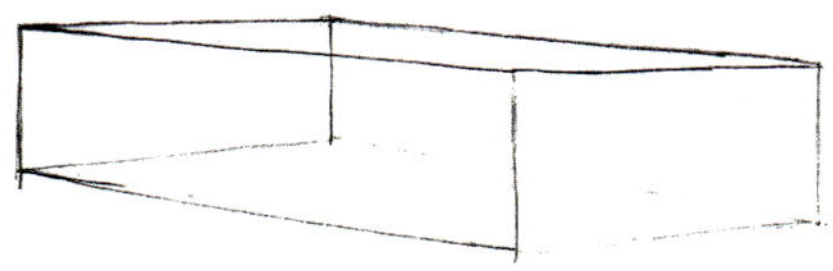

To start, draw a long 3-D box.

2

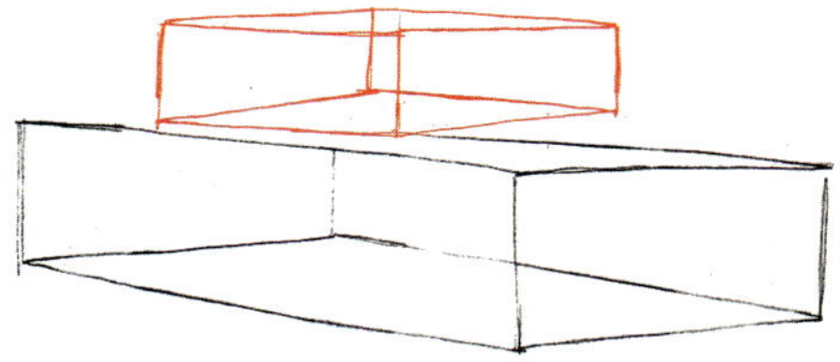

Next, draw a smaller box on top of the first one as shown in the illustration.

3

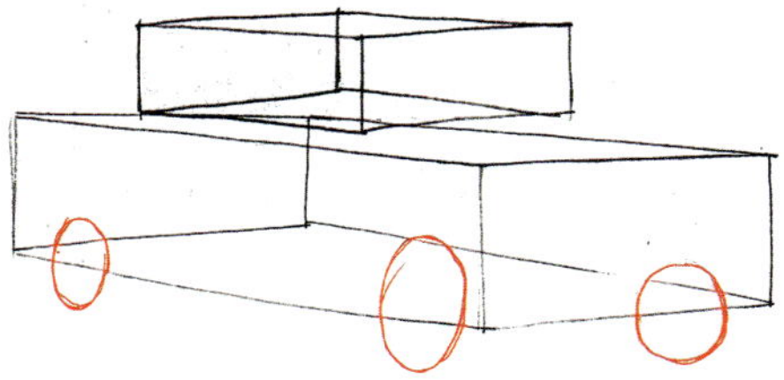

To make the wheels, draw three circles. Notice the size and placement of each circle.

4

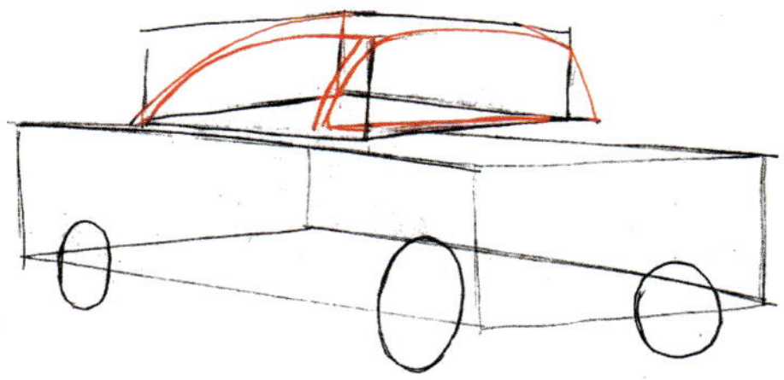

Then, draw the roof of the car by rounding off the top and sides of the top box. Draw curved rectangles to make the windows.

5

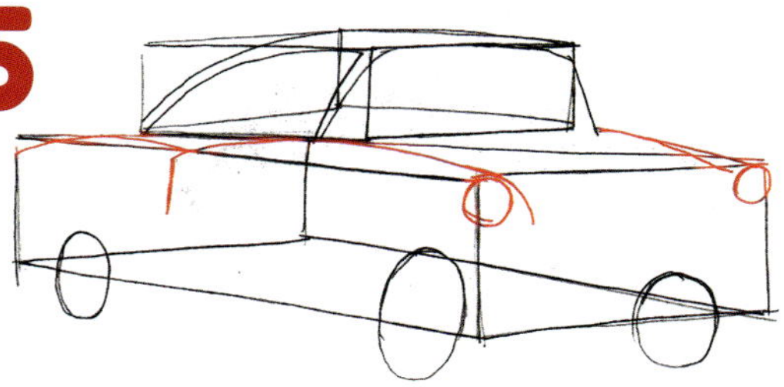

To shape the body of the Bel Air, add curved lines to the top of the bottom box. Now, draw two circles to the front of the bottom box to make the headlights.

6

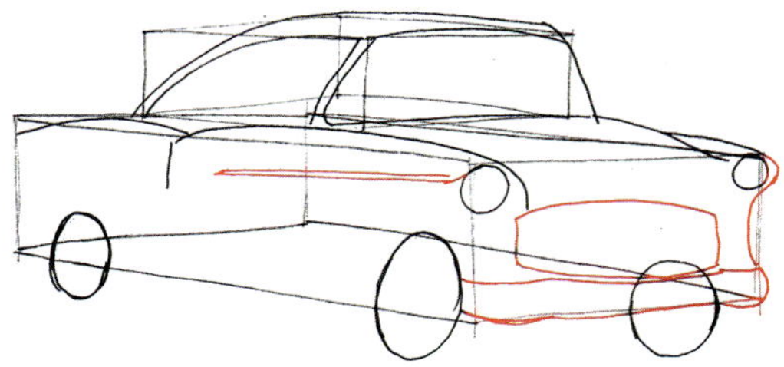

Draw a line along the side of the lower 3-D rectangle. Draw a rectangle with curved sides and a bumper on the front of the car. Curve the far side of the front as shown here.

7

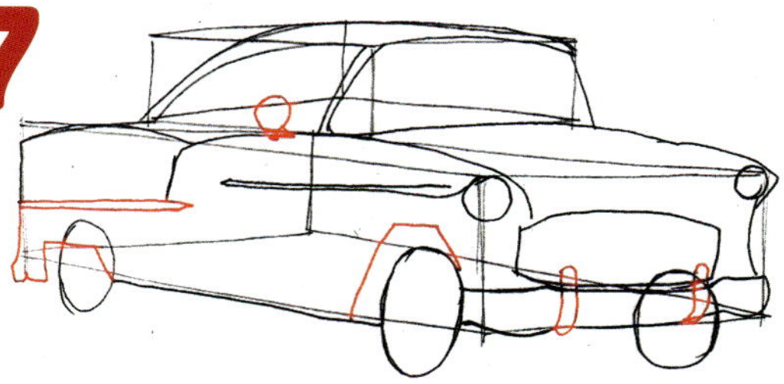

To make the rearview mirror, draw a small circle on the top of the side of the bottom box, near the middle. Draw a thin V shape starting at the back of the bottom box and ending in the middle. Add two small curved rectangles to finish the bumper, and add detailing to the back as shown here.

8

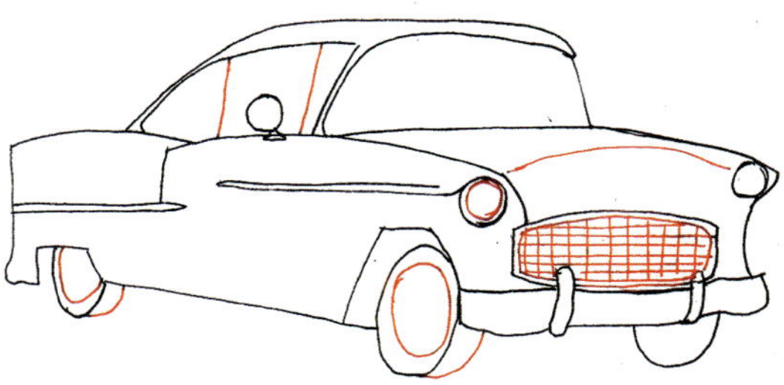

To make the windows, add two vertical lines. Draw a curved line at the top of the front side of the bottom box to make the hood. Add smaller circles inside the circles of the tires and headlights. Use horizontal and vertical lines to make the grille. Erase any extra lines. You've now made your own Bel Air Sport Coupe!

VOLKSWAGEN – THE PEOPLE'S CAR

The 1960s saw the rise of a new popular car in the United States—the Volkswagen. The model was nicknamed the "Beetle" because of its bug-like shape. It had a **controversial** history, though. In the 1930s, Austrian car designer Ferdinand Porsche and German Nazi leader Adolf Hitler wanted to make a car that all German people could afford, which led to this vehicle.

Eventually, the Volkswagen Beetle was brought to the United States from Germany. It was not very popular in the beginning because of its link with Hitler, but the car's low price soon made the Beetle a sensation. It was also nicknamed "the Bug" and was featured in a 1969 movie called *The Love Bug*.

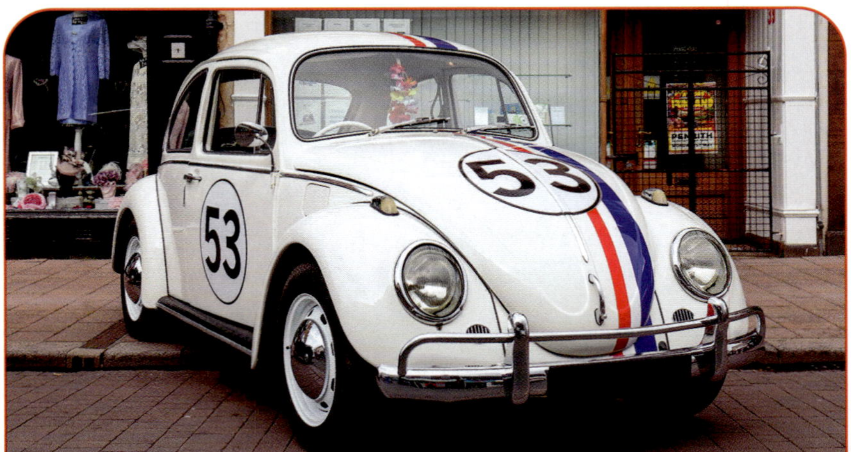

The Volkswagen, which in German means "people's car," was produced in Germany during World War II (1939–1945).

1

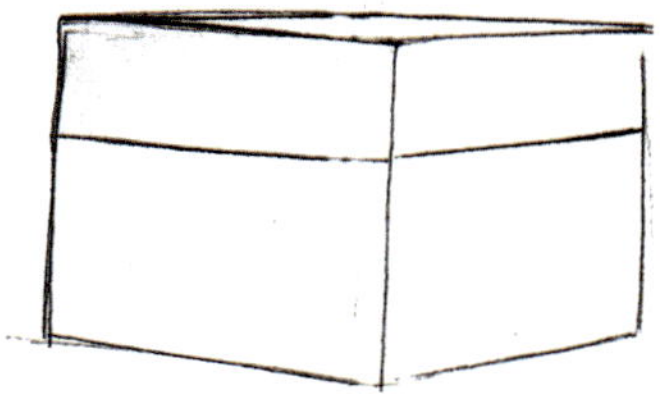

First, draw two 3-D rectangular boxes, one stacked on top of the other. This should look like a box with a lid.

2

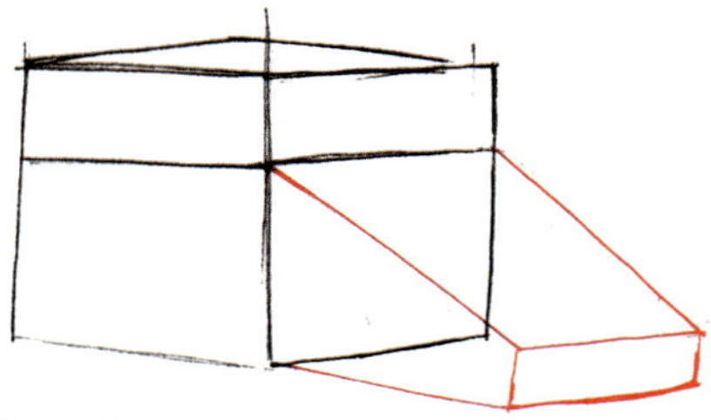

Next, extend lines from the box to create a 3-D triangle. Notice that the front end of the 3-D triangle is flattened.

3

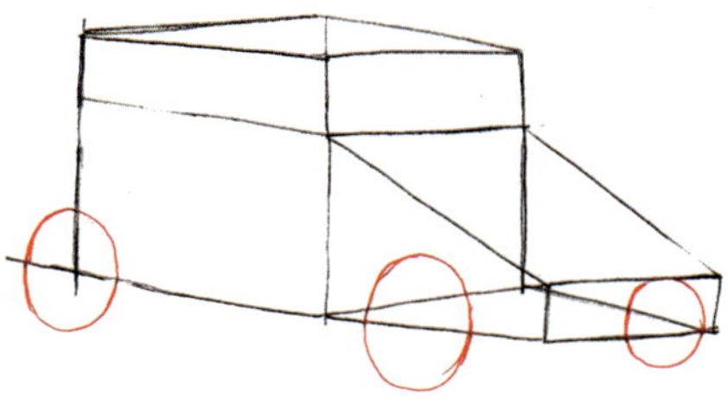

For the wheels, draw three circles. The circle farthest right should be smaller than the other two circles.

4

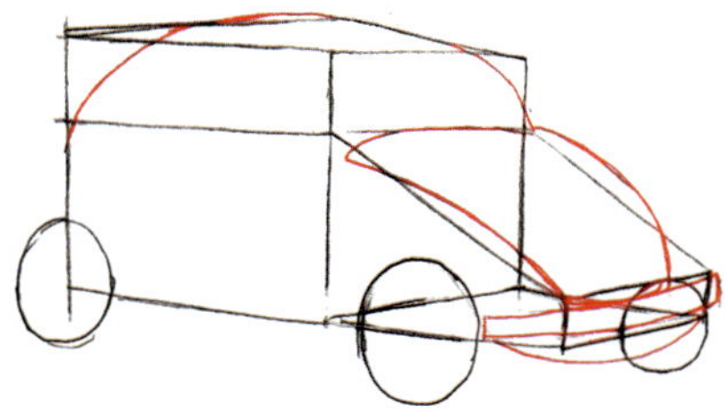

Round out the lines of the top of the box by curving the lines at the corners. Next, curve the lines on the tops and sides of the triangular shape.

5

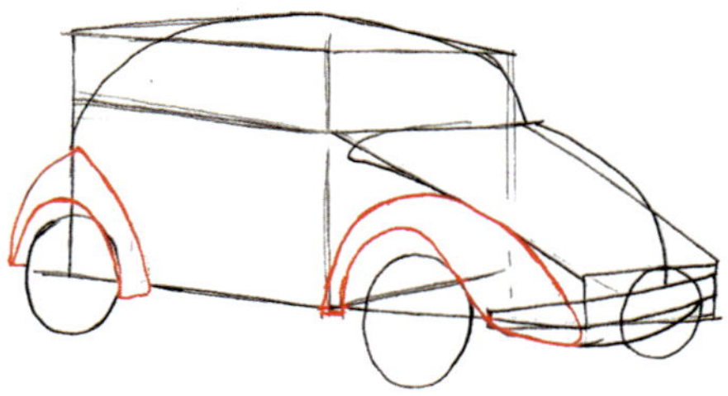

Then, draw curved lines halfway around the two largest wheels to make the fenders of the Beetle.

6

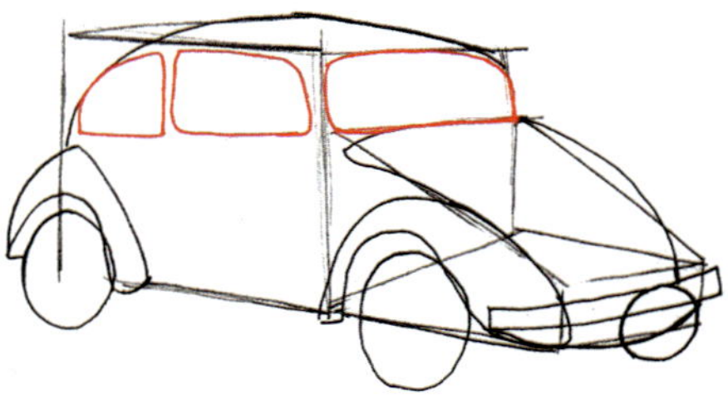

To make the windows, draw three rectangles in the lid of the box. Notice how each is a different size. Also, draw each rectangle with curved ends.

7

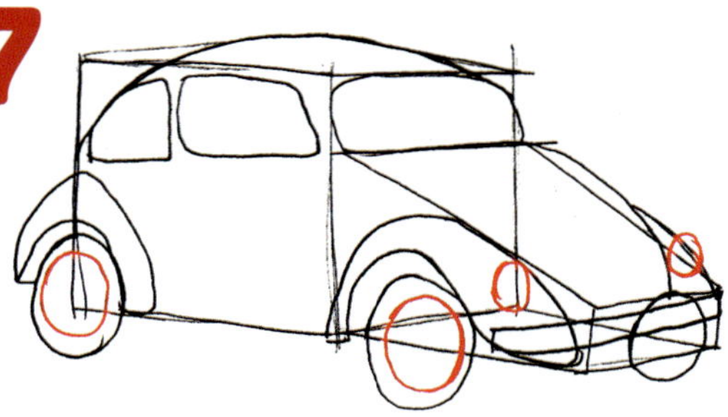

To make headlights, add two more circles to the front of the car. Then, draw two smaller circles inside the two larger circles that form the wheels.

8

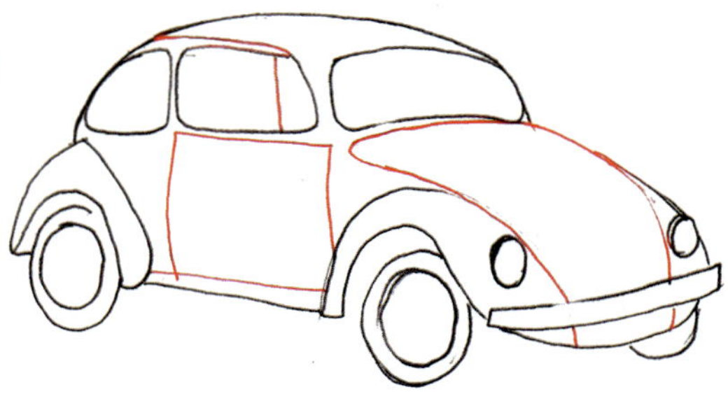

To make the car door, draw a square. Draw a vertical line in the middle window. Add curved details as shown here. Erase any extra lines. You've learned to draw a Volkswagen Beetle!

A SPEEDY SPORTS CAR

In 1962, the Shelby AC Cobra was the fastest sports car ever built. Its creator, Carroll Shelby gained a lot of experience and knowledge about cars from racing them. He was one of the first professional race car drivers but had to stop racing because of health issues. Then, he worked on making a car that had the body of a British AC Bristol sports car with an American Ford V8 engine.

The combination of the car's lightweight body and powerful engine helped it become a popular racing car. Early versions of the Shelby AC Cobra were clocked going from 0 to 60 miles (96.5 km) per hour in about 4 seconds. The V8 engine was the key to the Shelby AC Cobra's speed.

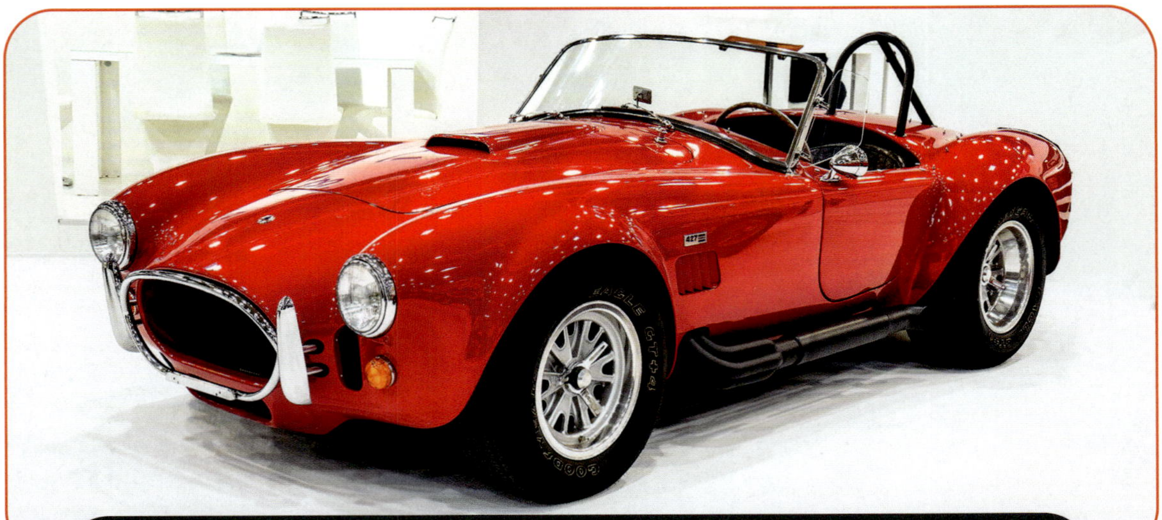

Between 1961 and 1968, fewer than 1,000 Shelby Cobras were built.

1

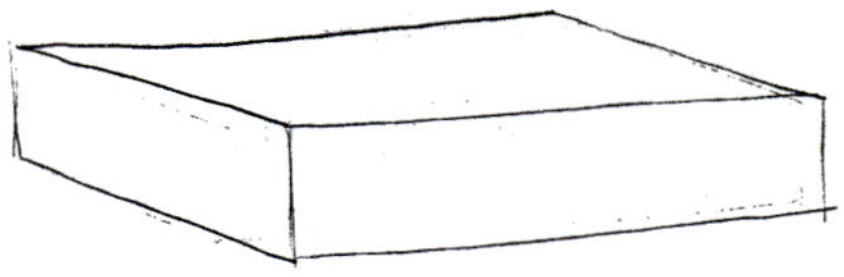

First, draw a flat, long box.

2

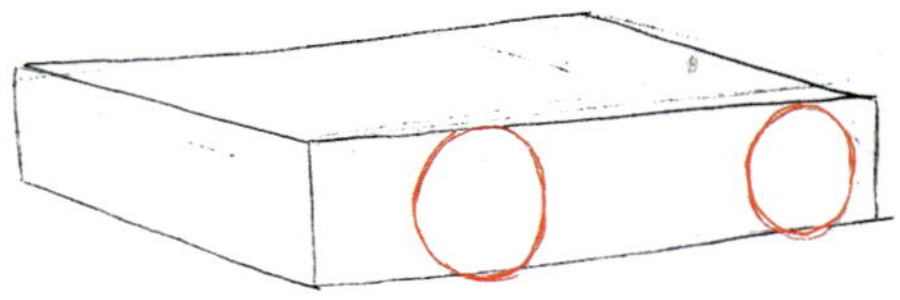

To make the wheels, draw two circles on one side of the box.

3

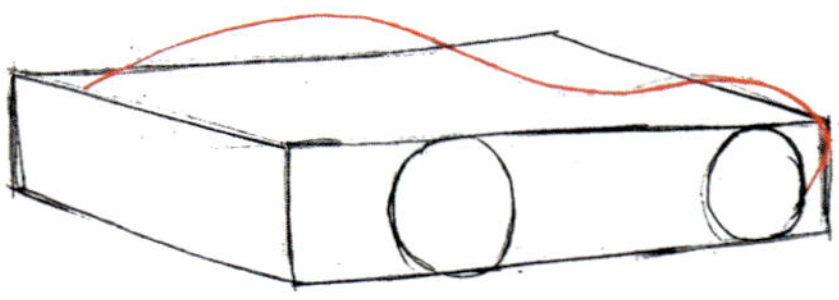

To make the body of the Shelby AC Cobra, draw a long, wavy line across the rectangle.

4

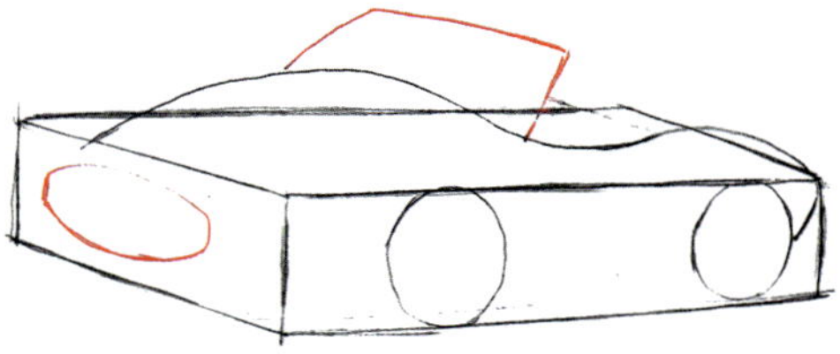

Next, form the windshield by drawing three sides of a rectangle on top of the curved line. Draw an oval on the smallest side of the box to make the grille. This is the front of the Shelby AC Cobra.

5

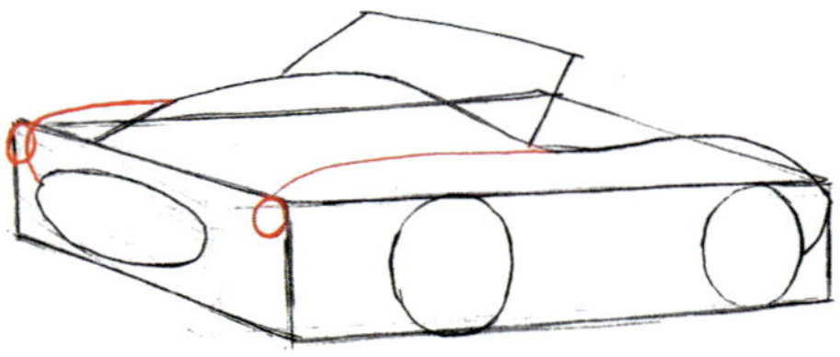

To make headlights, draw two small circles near the oval. Draw curved lines out from the headlights toward the back of the car.

6

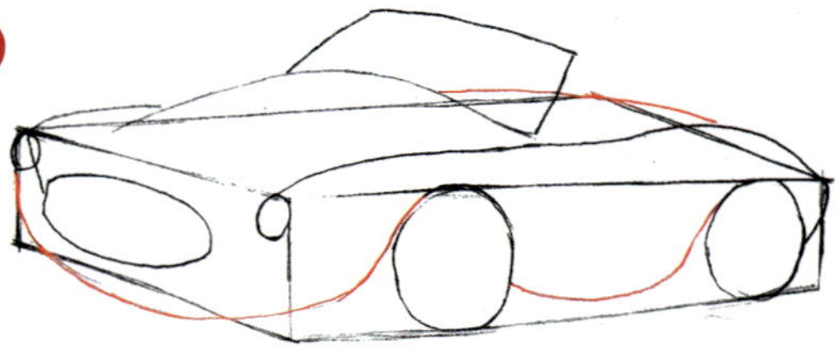

Draw a curved line from under the grille all the way to the back wheel. Then, draw a curved line behind the windshield.

7

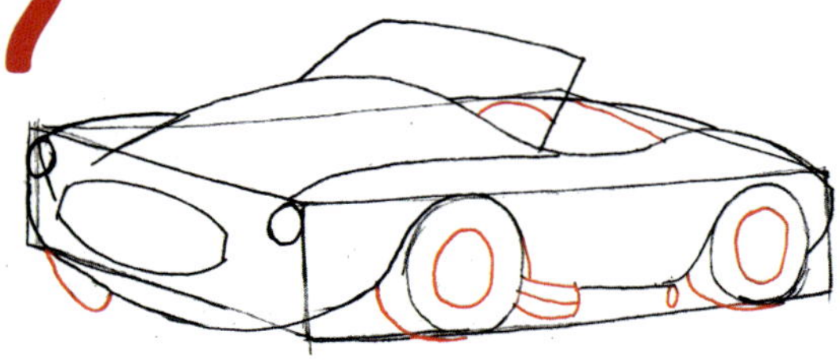

To make the tires, draw circles within the big circles. Draw a small curved line to make the steering wheel. Then, draw the exhaust pipe on the side and additional detailing as shown here.

8

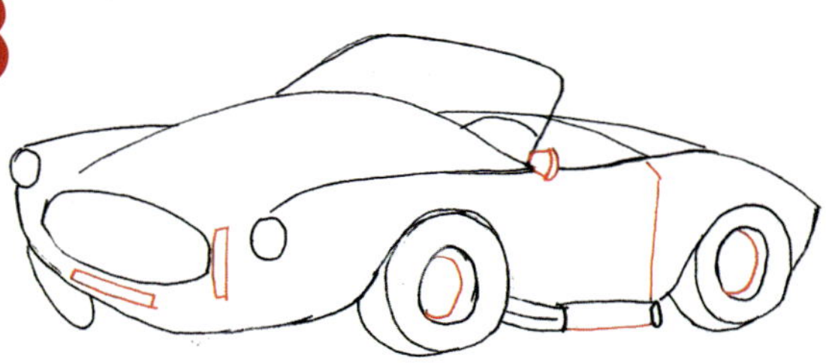

Next to the steering wheel, draw a rearview mirror. Add depth to the wheels by adding a curved line inside. Add a small thin rectangle underneath the grille. Erase any extra lines. You've now drawn a speedy Shelby AC Cobra!

A NEED FOR SPEED

The McLaren F1 is known as one of the fastest cars in the world. British race car designer Gordon Murray came up with the idea for the McLaren F1, and British designer Peter Stevens completed the final design. The average top running speed of the McLaren F1 is about 237 miles (381.4 km) per hour! That's double the top speed of most cars. In addition to being fast, the McLaren is expensive. It costs more than $1 million!

The McLaren is not popular as a car for everyday driving because many features have been taken out so the car can go fast. The McLaren is a great race car, though. In 1995, a McLaren F1 won the famous Le Mans 24-hour car race. It can go from 0 to 60 miles (96.5 km) per hour in 2.8 seconds.

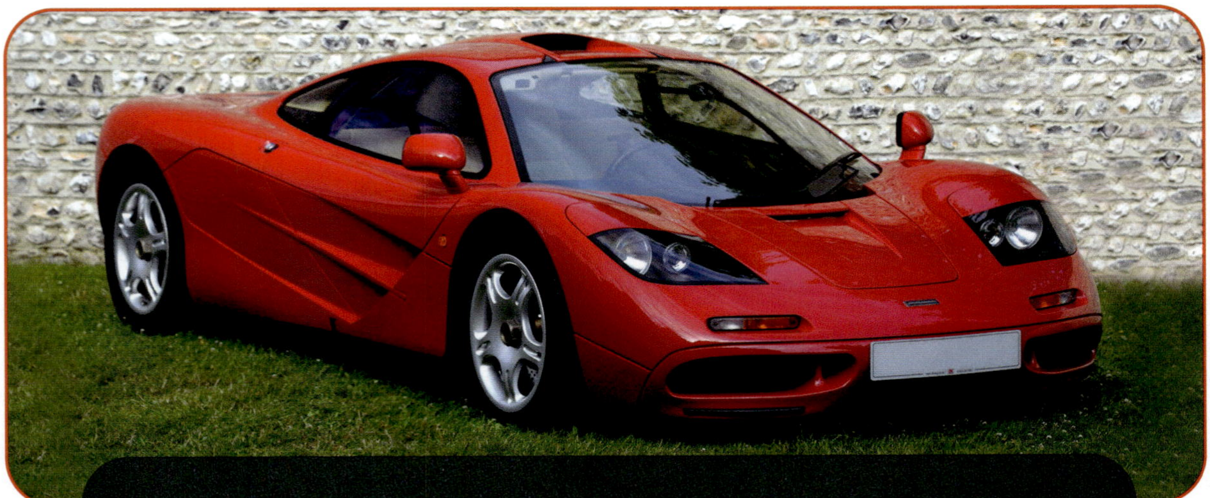

Only 106 McLaren F1 cars were ever produced. That makes it a very **exclusive** car.

1

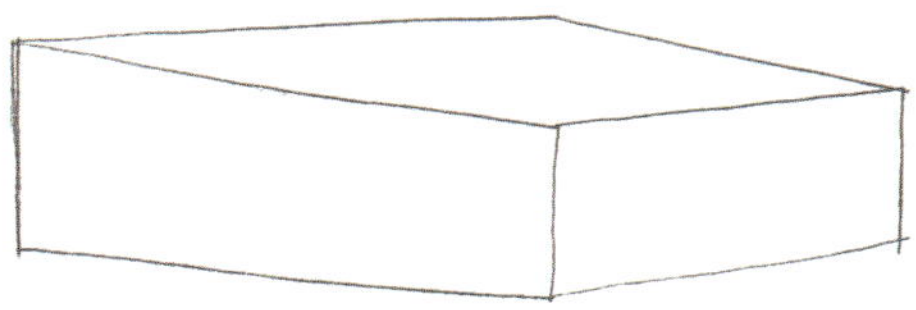

To start, draw a 3-D rectangle with the back slightly higher than the front.

2

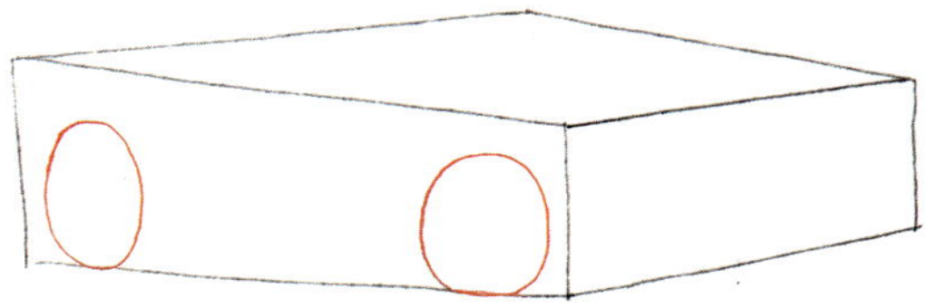

Next, draw two circles for the tires.

3

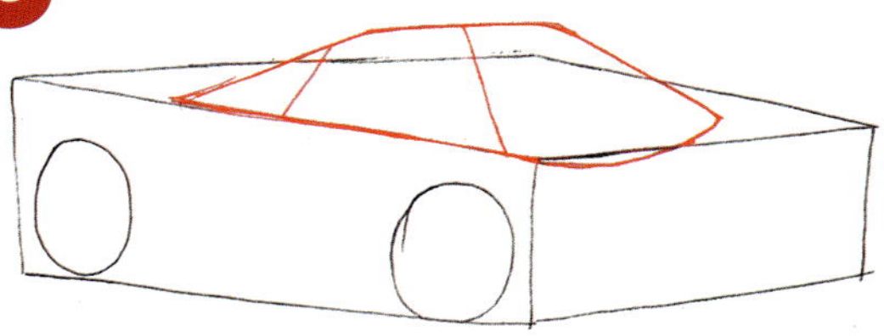

To make the roof, draw the shape shown on top of the rectangle. Next, draw two lines in this shape to begin forming the windows.

4

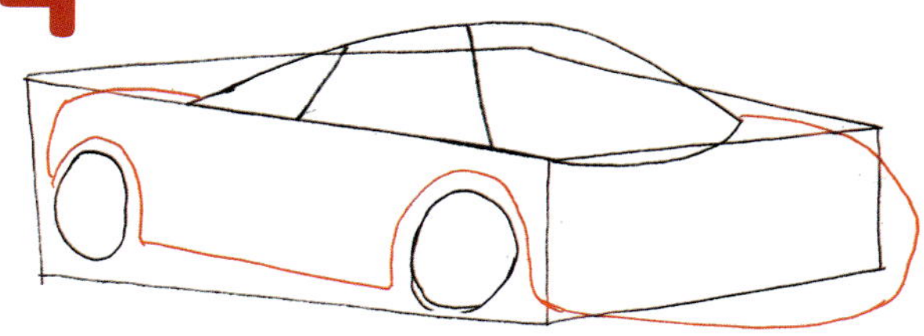

To make the body of the McLaren, make a curved line circling the car and going over the wheels as shown here.

5

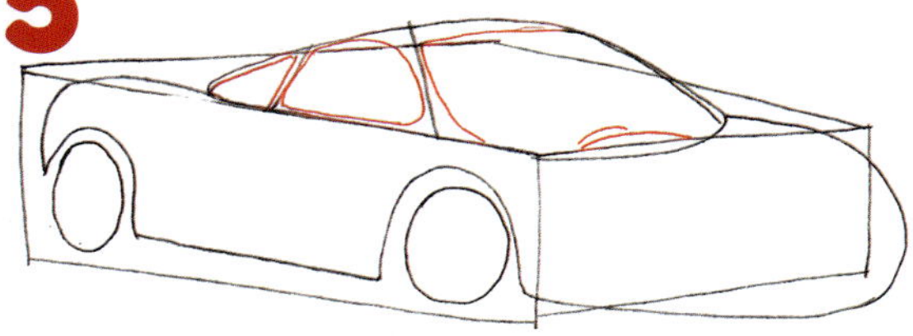

Then, draw the windows by making the shapes shown in the illustration. Draw two curved lines to make the steering wheel and dashboard.

6

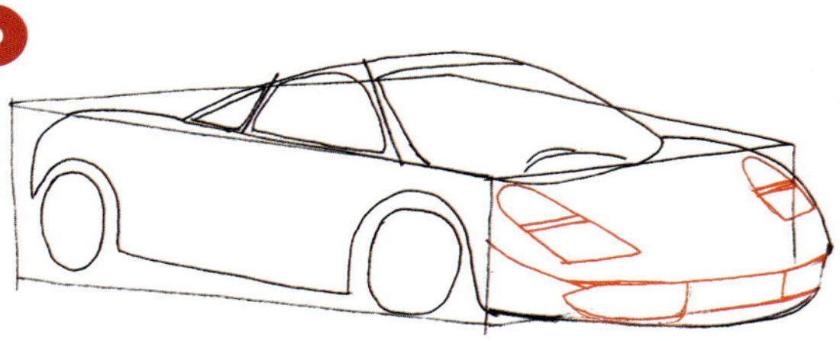

Draw the headlights to match the illustration above. Draw the bumper using curved horizontal lines.

7

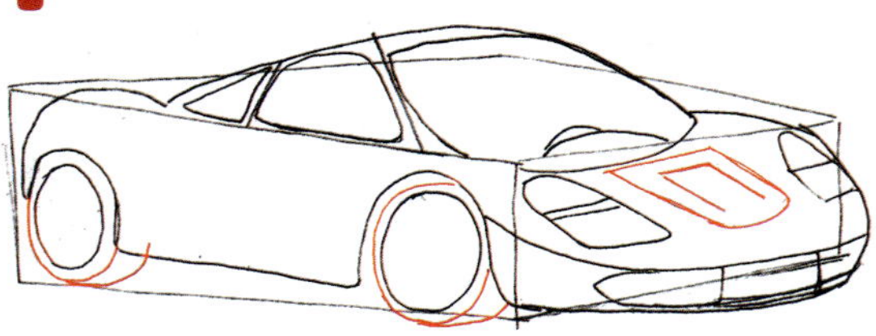

Now, draw the design on the hood of the McLaren. Add circles around the circles you drew in Step 2 to finish the wheels.

8

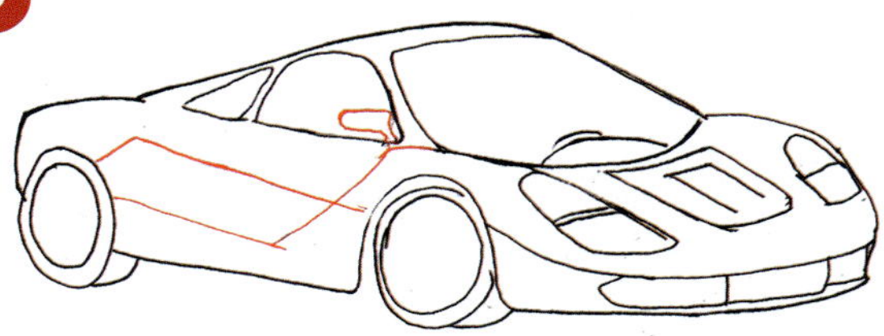

Lastly, add the rearview mirror. Draw the design lines on the side of the car. Clean up your drawing by erasing any extra lines. Your McLaren F1 is all done!

ON THE PROWL

After Amelia Earhart became the first woman to fly across the Atlantic Ocean as a passenger, she was given a Plymouth car. The Plymouth sports car was introduced in 1928 by the Chrysler Motor Company. The Plymouth was named after the colony in Massachusetts set up by the Pilgrims, who sailed from England on the Mayflower in the 1600s. The name links the car with the qualities of the settlers—strength, honesty, determination, and achievement.

In 1993, the Plymouth Prowler sports car was made public at the North American International Auto Show in Detroit, Michigan. The design was similar to the late 1930s classic American **hot rods**. By 1997, it was available to the public. It had a **retro** design with an exciting new aluminum body.

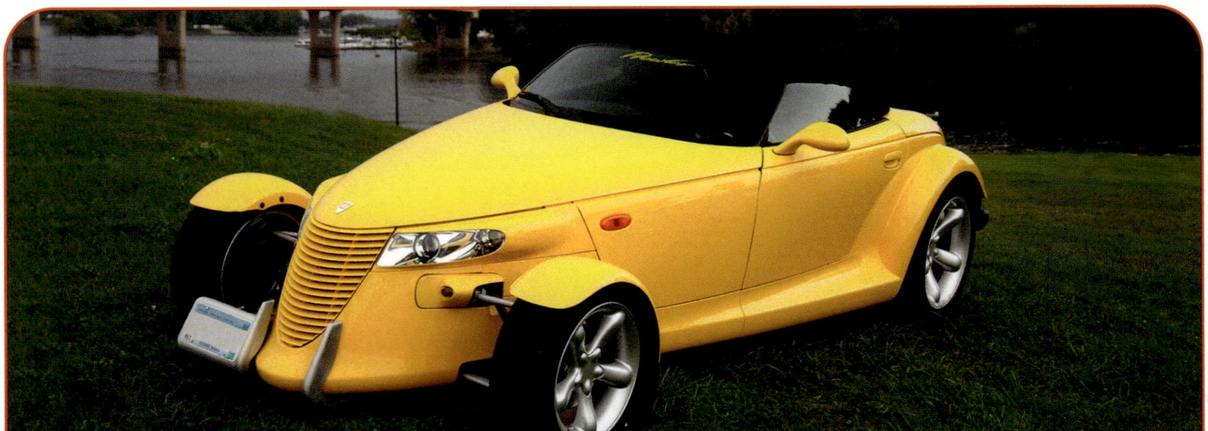

The body of the Prowler was made entirely of aluminum, which was very advanced for that time.

1

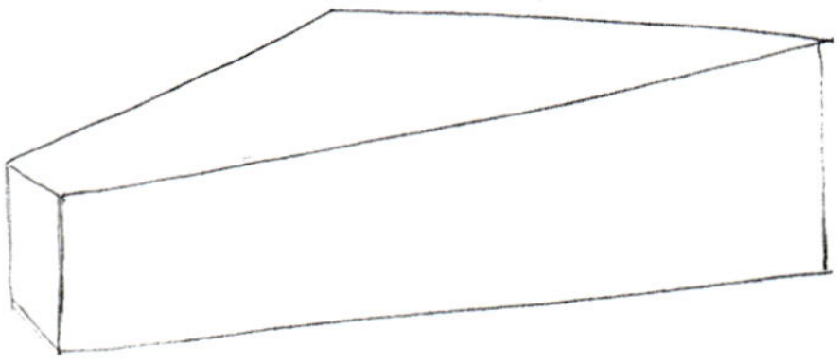

First, draw a box shaped like a triangle or wedge of cheese.

2

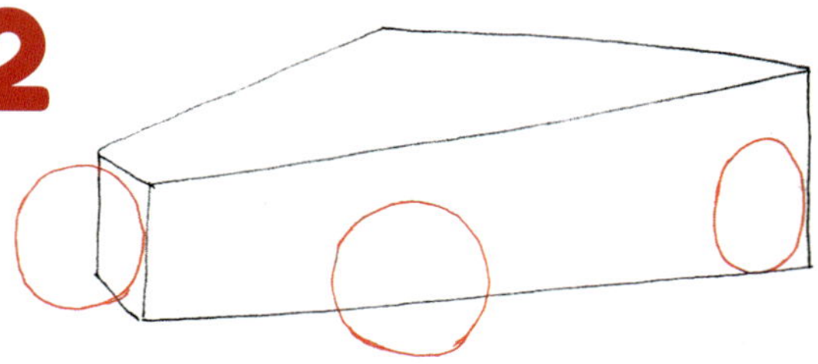

Now, draw three circles within the box. Look to the illustration to see their shape, size, and placement.

3

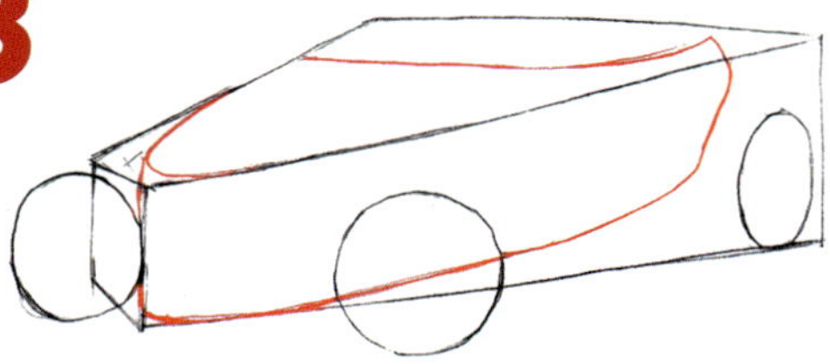

Next, make the body of the Prowler by drawing a curved shape inside the triangular shape.

4

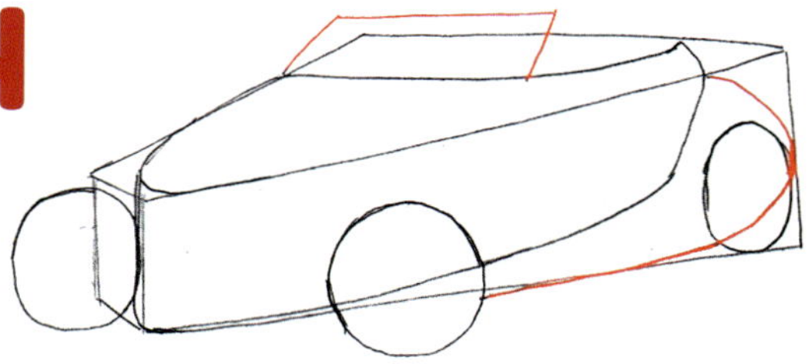

To make the windshield, draw a slanted rectangle. Draw a curved line beginning from the back of the Prowler and ending at the front tire.

5

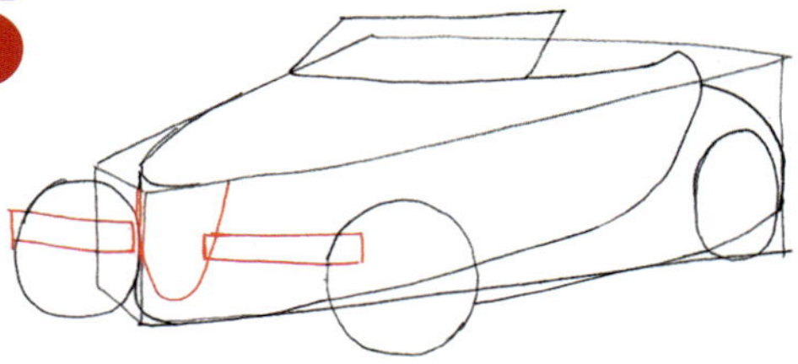

To make the bumper, draw two rectangles in the front. Draw a curved shape at the tip of the Prowler to make the grille.

6

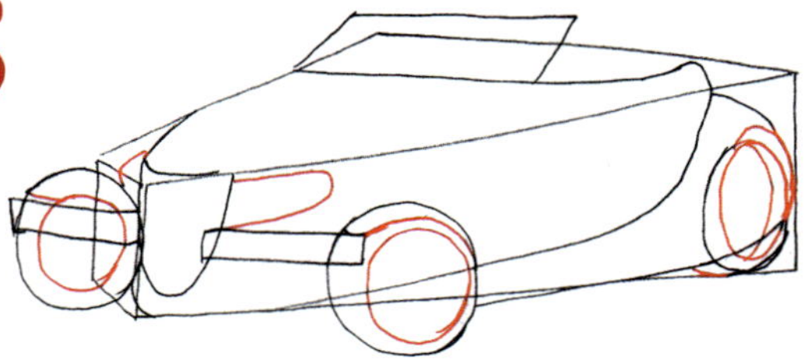

Draw circles within the circles of the tires. Then, draw a curved line from the grille.

7

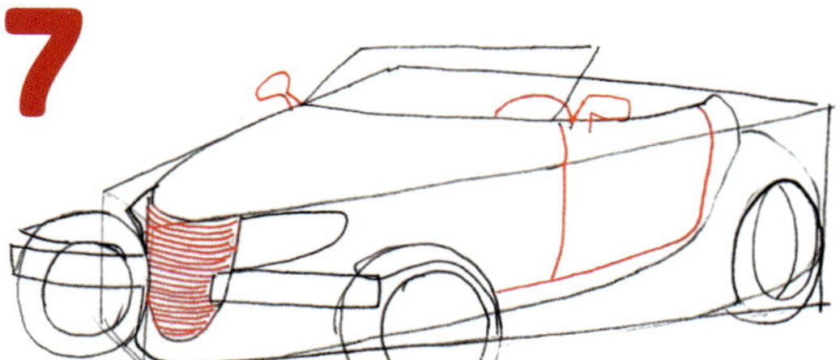

Add a curved line to create the steering wheel. Draw two lines for the doors. Draw the rearview mirrors on both sides. Lastly, add lines going across the grille for detail.

8

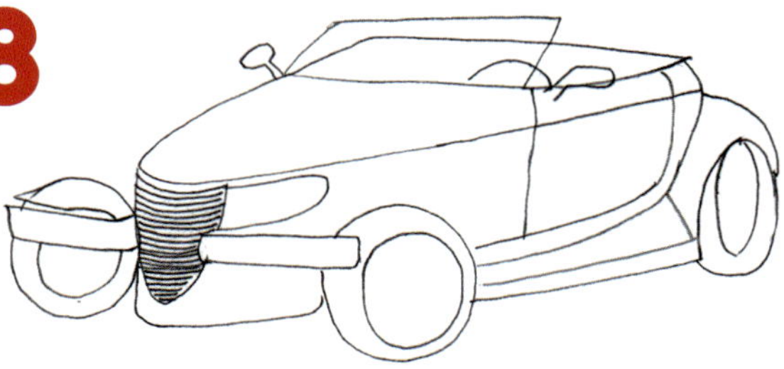

Clean up your picture by erasing any extra lines. You've finished perfecting your Plymouth Prowler!

GLOSSARY

assembly line: An arrangement of machines, equipment, and workers in which work passes down the line until the product is assembled.

controversial: Likely to create disagreement.

differential gear: An arrangement of gears in automobiles that allows the two wheels on a single axle to turn at different speeds. This helps when turning.

elegant: Having very high quality or richness of design.

engineer: Someone who plans and builds machines.

exclusive: Limiting possession, control, or use to a single person or group.

fender: Any of the corner parts of the body of a car, especially those that surround the wheels.

grille: A metal screen on the front of a car that allows cool air into the engine.

hot rod: An automobile rebuilt or modified for high speed and fast acceleration.

ignition: A device used to start a car.

luxury: Something rich and desirable but expensive or hard to get.

replica: A copy of something, exact in all details.

retro: Relating to styles and fashions of the past.

FOR MORE INFORMATION

WEBSITES

Henry Ford

www.ducksters.com/biography/henry_ford.php

Read more about Henry Ford's life, including his production process and the amazing Model T.

Most Popular Car

www.dkfindout.com/us/transportation/history-cars/most-popular-car/

Discover more about the Volkswagen Beetle, including a diagram of its parts.

BOOKS

Simons, Lisa M B. *Henry Ford*. North Mankato, MN: Capstone Press, 2019.

West, David. *Inside Cars*. New York, NY: PowerKids Press, 2018.

Publisher's note to educators and parents: Our editors have carefully reviewed these websites to ensure that they are suitable for students. Many websites change frequently, however, and we cannot guarantee that a site's future contents will continue to meet our high standards of quality and educational value. Be advised that students should be closely supervised whenever they access the internet.

INDEX